BARBLESS HOOKS AND ANCHORHOLDS

Other books by Benjamin Green:

The Field Notes of a Madman
encounters with reality
(personal essays)

Beyond Roses Are Red, Violets Are Blue
A practical guide for helping students write free verse
(nonfiction)

The Sound of Fish Dreaming   (poetry)

The Lost Coast   (poetry)

From a Greyhound Bus   (poetry)

BARBLESS HOOKS AND ANCHORHOLDS

by

Benjamin Green

Wood Thrush Books

Cover art by the author

Copyright c. 2004 by Benjamin Green
All rights reserved.

Printed by: Van Volumes
                Three Rivers, Massachusetts

Published by: Wood Thrush Books
                85 Aldis Street
                St. Albans, Vermont 05478

ISBN 0-9749334-5-7

INTRODUCTION

At first glance, *Barbless Hooks and Anchorholds* seems like a simple story about the joys of hiking and fishing in California's backcountry. Then the author speaks his mind. Ben Green's perception of the world is as unique as his approach to life, and both loom large in this narrative. When Ben recounts how he fished for years with hooks completely broken off, we realize that his is an unusual worldview. And from that point on, it becomes increasingly more apparent that this is a different kind of narrative – one that defies categorization.

In a word, this book is about starting points and standpoints which, by Ben's way of looking at things, are inexorably entwined. That is why language itself plays such a powerful role in the worldview sketched here, along with the methodology the author employs while hiking and fishing. That is why Ben's sense of impending doom, fed by the daily newspapers, must necessarily come to a head in the summer right before his 5-year-old daughter begins school.

When Ben introduces She'ifa to the wild that fateful summer, we get the feeling that it's now or never. We sense a growing tension between self and society as Ben points out the shortcomings of our educational system. Soon we find ourselves rooting for a man and his daughter, before we even know where this train of thought is taking us. When Ben describes in detail the natural history of the Russian Wilderness, we wonder if he's digressing. When he starts talking about the cultural history of the region, we're almost certain that he has strayed from the issue at hand. In due time, though, as Ben works his way deeper into the wilderness, moving closer to the *philosophical* heart of the matter, the pieces of the puzzle come together.

In the strictest sense, *Barbless Hooks and Anchorholds* is a work of fiction. Events did not occur exactly as they are portrayed here. In fact, the root of this narrative dates back to a trip into the Russian Wilderness that Ben took with his partner, Anita, before She'ifa was even born. And surely Ben's dark thoughts regarding the human condition had been stewing long before that. But these technicalities hardly matter. There is something in Ben's concern for his daughter that rings terribly true. It is a truth that many of us know all too well – a truth that makes this story a parable for our time.

Everything hinges upon whether or not Ben can provide his daughter with an anchorhold: a fixed reference point in a dangerous and ever-changing world. During the story, Ben makes it quite clear exactly where *he* stands on things. This he does through a series of ruminations that might seem to the inattentive as mere self-absorption. But Socrates would be proud. So would Thoreau, for that matter. In a world chock-full of true believers pushing their credos, it's refreshing to encounter a thinker whose beliefs aren't hyped, overstated or couched in half-truths. Fortunately for us, Ben enjoys fishing for truths as much as he enjoys fishing for trout – perhaps even more so.

– Walt McLaughlin

BARBLESS HOOKS AND ANCHORHOLDS

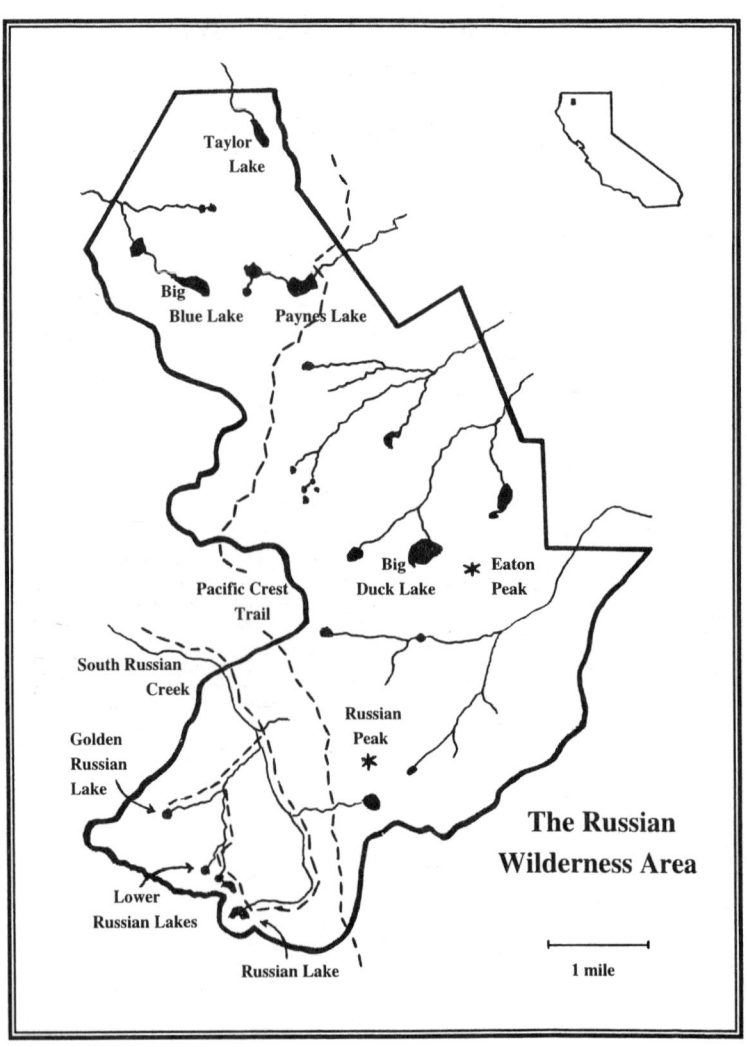

I. THE STARTING POINT: TRAILHEADS

And now it is June: the moon of the silver sky. Nothing is peaceful or rested. Blackberry vines swell powerfully. The very earth trembles with expectation. Parched grass quivers and tickles my feet. Newly arrived swallows, late this year, busily construct muddy nests on the undersides of the bridge that spans the creek. It is late spring: a time when the sunlight transforms itself into leaves and dances on the trees in the wind; a time when roots suck hard to reach the descending groundwater; a time for me to follow my daughter's shadow up from the flowing North Fork of the Salmon River to our campsite.

She'ifa has just turned five years old. We have spent the day in the mountains of northern California watching an unceasing, stinging northwind somersault maple leaves onto the rippled surface of the Salmon River. The air, already in motion at dawn, continued to stir without pause until this brief stilling, now, at sunset.

It has been a silent spring day, as well; songbirds were compelled to roost from daybreak to eventide. It seems only with luck that in the calm twilight they manage to pull a song of distress from their empty purses before they frantically take evening flights for food.

I am as unsettled as the rest of the world, but this is June and She'ifa is five years old, so the mood seems apt. I came to let my thoughts drift far toward meaning and consequence, and sift back to me, toward origins and sources. I came to let my mind, my life, flow like the river, to let my worries drift away on the water's current. She'ifa came to be with her father, and to play. We spent the afternoon in the water, and now it is time to return to camp.

It is June. Away briefly from my job as a school janitor, I am here in a mood between fatigue and despair. It is not the job that causes the feeling, although I admit to looking forward to my "time off" with relief and joy. I intentionally do not use the word "vacation." "To vacate" would imply a need to pursue diversions, a need to get away from my normal everyday life and self to find some happiness.

It is June and I am overwhelmed by an anxiety and sadness that was brought on by a simple subscription to the daily newspaper. And, of course, I am constantly reminded that She'ifa is five. That means this is the last summer before school *starts* for my daughter.

Yet, how often I was told that the world will *end* . . .

Science teachers taught that the sun would burn out. Some climatologists promised a return of the ice; others warned of rising oceans and death by drowning. Population experts predicted that people would outbreed the food supply. There are already 6 billion of us, with no hope of slowing the growth rate until we total 7 billion, and of those it is promised that a quarter will live in "absolute poverty" while at least a tenth will be starving. Humans have "wasted" a fifth of the earth's topsoil and a sixth of the total farmland in just the last forty years. Educated experts stood on every corner of my youth with pickets raised announcing "the end is coming soon."

These experts were convincing and I was certain they were correct, but their predictions were positioned as far, or further, in the future as the dinosaurs were in the past.

But, now, I am almost 45 years old and I read daily where the end of the world seems too near. The newspaper's description of human affairs promises "the end" to be much closer to tomorrow than to a million years hence. The destruction that is being foretold is usually not dramatic; it is the strangely comforting numbness of a toxic mire. The world, it seems, will not end with a bang but in a fester.

And now it is June. As She'ifa and I walk along the banks of the Salmon River, the wind's cold fingers and hard lips touch us again. The sky is silver. The river ripples and blackens granite stones in a pebbly clatter. Insect larvae flash in the moving water. The shoreline rises steep and fast, a sheer wall wedged over the creek like a slipping weight. The slope is crumbly, thin-skinned, but crowned to the ridge tops with raucous growth that conceals vertiginous views.

On the dirt road that leads to the trailhead we see dust curling behind a few trucks and cars like wool on sheep. The leaves on the roadside are powdered, waiting for the distant fall rains to wash them clean again. A wild and frightening beauty rests up there.

The field next to the campground is full of hoary thistles beginning to flower. These weeds are yellow and purple-haired, wig-headed invaders. They usually attract a charm of finches, but this is a windy June and the birds are stuck in their roosts.

This is the landscape I have come to fish. Up that dusty road is the trailhead to the Russian Wilderness, an area encompassing a small granite ridgeline containing several small lake basins. I have heard of a lake and the rumor of golden trout. But I am not here for the fish as much as for the land.

When people ask me why I fish, I tell them, "For the landscape." They ask, "Is the landscape so great when you *don't catch* fish?" Then I know I am talking to someone who does not understand.

There was a stretch of years after I first learned to fly cast when I broke off the entire hook on my flies. Seeing the fish rise to my offering was enough. I had to endure the advice of experts telling me how to "set a hook." I lasted out the doubting glances, head-shakings, and lots of laughter when I showed my hook-less flies.

I enjoy catching and even eating an occasional fish, but that is not the reason I fish. Fishing is the excuse to get me into the landscape. The landscape remains the goal: the lake and the river and everything connected to them. The fish are there and, yes, I can catch them sometimes, and I am glad for that.

I fish for the many myriad landscapes that water creates. When I fish for rainbow and brook trout, I happen to be in a wet beauty that conspires to make all of nature a seduction. Trout, especially wild trout, are connected to distinctive landscapes and it is these landscapes and the experience of them that I have learned to covet.

For me the word *trout* includes insects, the sound of moving water, the reflections on still water, and trees and light, and other forms of wildlife, and the experience of solitude. These are all good things, and in those unfortunate places where the trout have been lost, there is still much of value to be found.

The watching hills that surround She'ifa and me contain many good things: the scent of dogwood suddenly beside a rocky spring creek, the glimmer of the stars on granite, the morning song of a water ouzel . . .

One of the reasons I have come here is in hope that She'ifa will have the strength to remain herself when school starts in August. She is only five and has not yet learned how difficult it is to remain her self in a public setting. She will have to be able to resist the brutalization that our public schools call socialization. She will need many personal interests to overcome the urge to compromise. She chose ballet as a passion. She has gymnastics and martial arts. I want to offer her fishing as an anchorhold, as another way to hold steady.

The Russian Wilderness seems a good place to make the introduction. Playing in the water today, She'ifa seemed interested in the rocks. I explained to her that most of the stones were granite, that granite contains gold and chromite, and that the glaciers that carved this landscape also deposited minerals into the rivers. I told her our campground, where the South Russian meets the Salmon, was once a mining camp.

The Russian Wilderness Area is located in the Klamath Province, a geological region in sharp contrast to the rest of the state of California. The rocks here are older than those found in the coastal ranges to the west, in the Cascades to the east, and in the Sierra Nevada to the south. The rocks in the Klamath, near Scott Mountain and China Peak, in particular, are some of the oldest to be found on earth, made some 500 million years ago.

Individual samples of rocks within this wilderness are deformed and metamorphosed, warped and faulted.

The entire province is likewise twisted, for the same forces that made the rocks shaped the larger landscape.

The mix of rock paints an impressionistic canvas: marbles are off-white, granites are black and white with various shades of pink, the volcanic rocks are red, the serpentine is green, and the schist is blue.

The mountains in the Klamath are younger than the rocks they are made of. The range that contains the Russians was created by a major episode of folding. The granite ridgelines appeared later, much later. These granite intrusions, known as plutons, shouldered aside the older rock. Geologists describe how magma was forcefully injected into the metamorphic zone in two pulses, one liquid and one solid. The granite consolidated during its upward movement, crystallizing at borders and margins, rupturing and granulating.

This granite has been subject to glaciation, as well. Compared to the birthing of the Klamath province rocks, compared to the creation of the mountains, the glaciation was a recent event. Most of the lakes in the Russians were formed only 10,000 years ago, when ice carved out basins in the bedrock. The rivers of this water-shaped earth, the Scott and Salmon, originated in the same episodes of glaciation (The Klamath River for which the region was named, interestingly enough, is older than the mountains it flows through. The river existed *before* the mountains).

The result of this geological activity is a structurally complex region. Bold, dark and gathering mountains flank so steep they could be called cliffs. Thousands of deep and narrowly trenched nameless canyons are invigorated with streams. Countless broad ridges, great crests and pine-clad hills reach out in all directions blocking views and catching clouds. Sharp peaks, contoured by glaciers, tower over U-shaped cirques with bedrock basins, lakes, and marshy meadows. The ice fields and glaciers created horns, aretes, glacial troughs and stairways, waterfalls, tarns, moraines, and hanging canyons.

One such glacially carved valley holds South Russian Creek. At the headwaters of one fork of the creek is Golden Russian Lake. I have heard that it is a little and unassuming mid-elevation pond. I have also heard rumors that it was planted with golden trout, making it one of the few places in northwestern California where I can angle for the state fish. Their scientific name is *Oncorhynchus mykiss aguabonita*, the last part meaning "beautiful water." Right now, in June, they should be splendid in their spawning colors. This knowledge has kept me going all spring in anticipation.

The Klamath is a strange landscape: a succession of ridges and peaks, a world not made by humans, a world that precedes humans, a world so wild and old that it may go beyond human understanding and knowing, but not beyond the human ability to experience. It is a landscape too complex and tortured to surrender itself to concise or summary description. Thus, it is a great place to get lost, and a good place to go fishing.

I fish in places like the Russian Wilderness because, there, through fishing, I regain the experience of being connected. Fishing in the wilderness, fishing in an intact ecosystem, allows me to participate. Angling is a form of direct contact with the wild world: fundamental, original and elemental. In one act, water, air, stone, darkness and light, heat and cold are all involved. My line is an arachnid thread that binds me to the world, to the wild, to the wild that is left inside me.

I have found that the sense of a place is easier to find, easier to discover, if I go to the water, and follow its lead. Water, a lake or even a moving river, is a point of fixity, a vantage-point, a point of reference, and a standing point. It is a starting point, a point of entry. Water locates, situates.

Water weaves; one thing leads to another. Vectors of ascent and descent converge. In a strange landscape, new and unfamiliar, water is a good place to start the process of discovery and exploration because water draws all things to itself. It allows access; it is an approach.

Then, when I catch a fish, there is physical evidence that I have gained some understanding of a place. Fishing is about *relationships*. Water relates to weed, weeds relate to protozoa, protozoa relate to insect larvae, larvae relate to hatch, hatches relate to fish, fish relate to eagle, eagle relates to tree, trees relate to rock spires, rock spires relate to sky, sky relates to moon, moon relates to sun and stars ...

Through fish, through the act of fishing, I connect to all of that. I become woven within the rest of Creation. Fishing is part of my work in finding the meaning of the universe. Geometry and gravity converge in this sport to create a universe that is the sum of subjective relationships.

Fishing's narrow focus screens out distractions and diversions. I get an angle on the true subject. Fishing is the crossing of lines, vectors of fish and lure hopefully meeting. These converging lines create patterns of relationships. Follow the tip of my fly rod and that is all I see: patterns everywhere. *Everywhere.*

Gravity works on water. Water falls and flows; tides ebb and flood; streambeds are dry in the morning and then wet in the afternoon. A river is nothing but gravity and fluidity joined as one, joined, and then split at the same time. Unity and plurality are married.

When a fish rises, creates a ripple that expands in circles across a lake, it is easy to see that everything is a wave. *Everything.*

When I watch a river flow past in small waves, it is also easy to believe that the universe itself is nothing more or less than a *stream* of possibility, potential, and particularity.

With the focused concentration required while fishing, I always seem to catch *something*, if not fish. I do not *know* much about weeds and protozoa, insects and fish, eagles and trees, but through fishing I have gained some understanding of them. I have gained some understanding of the places that are created by these interrelationships. I think that is the true meaning of *ecology*.

The womb of geology, the secret of how the landscape crystallized, is one standpoint, one way to look at and to describe the Russian Wilderness Area. Another perspective is the geographic.

In the time of author Herman Melville, perhaps one could say that true places could not be found on any map. In the first years of the Twenty-first Century, however, a current and reliable map is helpful for finding the ends of the road where the real world begins.

For the Russian Wilderness Area, in particular, the following are necessities: a current map, an understanding of the Forest Service's peculiar road numbering system, and updated personal advice from a ranger or from another hiker who is familiar with and who has recently explored the area.

There are more than 100 miles of logging roads in the French Creek watershed alone. There are an additional 80 miles of skid trails in this same drainage on the east slope of the Russian Wilderness. This mileage of dirt track may explain why over 80,000 tons of silt eroded annually from the granite soils of French Creek into the Scott River until recent controls were implemented. Although most of these roads have been closed, and some of them serve as trails in the new wilderness, enough remain open to confuse both the newcomer and the experienced. Visitors to the wilderness should come prepared to enter a dusty maze.

The Russian Wilderness Area is a federally designated wilderness within the Klamath National Forest in Siskiyou County, California. Designated in 1984 by the California Wilderness Act, the area is 12,000 acres in size. The main spine of the wilderness is comprised of the Russian Mountains (referred to as the *Salmon Mountains* on some older maps). Russian Peak, the high point of the area, reaches 8196 feet. The lower reaches of the preserve begin at 5000 feet in old growth forest. The wilderness contains 22 named lakes in glacial basins. The headwaters of the Scott and Salmon rivers and their tributaries comprise the major watersheds.

The Klamath Province is not only geologically unique, it is also one of the most diverse ecosystems in North America. It supports the second most ecologically diverse forest in the United States. The complexity of vegetative patterns is due to the variety of rocks and soils.

Plant life contributes to the colorful canvas of the Klamath. Peridotite and serpentine are rocks from deep within the earth's mantle. They do not release calcium, a necessity for plant growth. The few plants that do grow in these kinds of soils are usually gray, not green. The granite soil, in contrast, hosts a raucous diversity of dark green plants. Some of the alpine and volcanic soils have no plant life. Add botany to geology and the canvas begins to look more abstract and expressionistic.

The diversity of trees in this low elevation maritime mountain system was a major factor in earning wilderness designation. A single square mile of forest surrounding Russian Peak contains 17 different species of conifers. This is a North American, and perhaps world, record.

Western yew, prostrate juniper, incense cedar, mountain hemlock, Engelmann spruce, weeping spruce, Douglas fir, white fir, Shasta red fir, subalpine fir, white bark pine, sugar pine, western white pine, foxtail pine, lodgepole pine, Jeffrey pine, and ponderosa pine are all present. 450 other non-conifer plant species are also present.

Many factors contribute to this diversity. The wild beginnings of the region's geology left a legacy in the biology of this wilderness, especially in the botany.

The many soil types in the Klamath are discontinuous. In places, granite soil exists in the same watershed alongside serpentine and peridotite. In other locales, volcanic rock rests on top of fertile sediment. There is little evidence of a pattern. The varying amounts of moisture in these different soil types add another important component to vegetation type and contribute to even greater diversity.

The soil in the Klamath has been disturbed enough to create complexity but not enough to destroy relic populations. The Klamath is what is known as a "refugium," or a place of refuge for plant species. Plants exist here that once were common everywhere else before Pleistocene glaciation. Modern conifers that appeared in the late dinosaur age are very common in the Russian Wilderness. The weeping spruce, also known as Brewer's spruce, is found only in the Klamath province. It is a tree that is shade tolerant and prefers a north-facing slope. This spruce is a relic species from the Miocene and Pliocene epochs; that is, it is a tree that has existed for 25 million years. Other species remnant of a truly ancient past, such as Eocene epoch plants from 40 million years ago, still grow in the Russian Wilderness.

Along South Russian Creek, which leads to Golden Russian Lake, the climate today is similar to what it was 40 million years ago. Fifty inches of rainfall a year is common; snow falls above the 4000-foot elevation (with amounts ranging from 5 to 20 feet per year). Most winters are not particularly harsh, but a rough winter leaves its scars.

Summers, similar to 40 million years ago, are hot, with 60-degree temperature variation from day to night being common. Although thunderstorms frequent summer afternoons, for the most part summer is a time of drought.

The diversity of Klamath botany is a result of both relics (older species no longer present elsewhere because climates changed over epochs) and mixing (species common to the Cascades, the Sierra Nevada, the Modoc Plateau, and the coast are also present in the Russian Wilderness). This rich botanical garden is not orderly but all mixed together.

There are nine different plant communities present in the Russians. There are *mixed evergreen, lowland forests* on the west side along the untouched and unnoticed South Russian Creek. The dense and extensive riparian stands in this classic, glacially carved U-shaped valley show the greatest vegetative diversity in a pristine condition in the nation. *Mixed conifer forests* grow at most of the trailheads and along lower elevation trails. *Red fir forest*, cold and high, dark and dripping with gray moisture, surrounds most of the lakes. *Sub-alpine* forests grow at timberline or on granite ridges and cliffs. *Mountain meadows* surround many of the lakes, especially where inlet creeks fill the basins. *Montane chaparral* covers a large portion of the west side, high elevation, sun-drenched slopes. *Alpine fell fields* exist where the snow piles high and prostration becomes the prevalent plant survival strategy. There are also *streamside plant communities* and *ultramafic soil plant communities* present in the Russian Wilderness. The list makes it sound simple, but all these communities are mixed together in the wilderness, making it a tangled garden.

Fire has also helped to shape the botanical diversity in the wilderness. The Klamath region and the Russians in particular are subject to a high frequency of low intensity fires. These fires have helped to create multi-aged stands of various tree species.

Humankind has helped to shape the biology of the wilderness, as well; logging and mining have had their impacts. Logging created artificial "edges" within plant communities. Salvage logging of wildfire burned habitats has slowed recovery because nitrogen fixing herbs and shrubs were not allowed to regenerate. Early logging methods did not allow for tree reproduction and large brush fields were created. This is evident on the road up French Creek. Logging appears to have also changed the climate. Snowfall on Etna Mountain has averaged 38% less since the heavy cuts of the 1970s and 1980s.

Mining left piles of tailings and shaft spoils, most of which are toxic and sterile. After a century of weathering, these wastelands still support no plant life.

Interestingly, the diverse plant life in the Klamath is not especially accommodating to animal life. Snails and slugs, myriapods (many-legged crawlers), scorpions, salamanders, shrews, mountain beavers, and bats are some of the more common animals in the Russian Wilderness. It is no surprise that these are also very old and primitive species. They have existed along with the forest since its inception. The birds, squirrels, deer, bear, or the animals we commonly associate with the forest, are newcomers. Because of the prevalence of forest in the wilderness, and because these are pristine forests, the Russians are home to many rare species: fisher, marten, wolverine, pileated woodpeckers, goshawks, and, of course, many species of fish: steelhead trout, salmon, golden trout . . .

There are many ways to describe the Russian Wilderness. There are many ways to go fishing. Fishing has been a perennial human preoccupation (or occupation); even *pre*-humans fished, using their hands, feet and teeth. Those were the original, or aboriginal, tools for catching and gathering fish.

Sometimes when I am bored having bad luck attracting fish out from under cutbanks with a fly or lure, I will put my hands under the bank, feel around in the tree roots, and maybe scare a trout with my fingers. So, hand gathering still occurs, but I do not know much about fishing with my feet or teeth.

Some fishermen dive for fish, capturing them with spears, or grabbing them with their hands after attracting them with bait. Again, in times of boredom or bad luck, I have lunged after visible trout with my pole tip. It gets a rise out of the same fish that have been ignoring me all day, and I guess it gets a rise out of me as well. The Shasta Indians sometimes speared fish in the lakes and rivers of the Russian Wilderness. It is a practice beyond my patience.

Some cultures, in the Orient especially, have trained other animals to catch fish for human consumption. For example, cormorants, slim-necked fish-eating birds, catch fish for their human masters. The sleek black birds are stopped from swallowing the fish by a ring around their throats and are forced to regurgitate the fish they catch. I have read where Irish and Scottish tribes trained otters in the same way, but I do not know how they kept the critters from eating their fish.

Some people stupefy fish, stunning them with poison or electroshock or even dynamite. Some use a spear, a harpoon, or a gun to catch fish. I have seen people shoot at trout. The water causes the light to bend so the fish are not where they appear to be. The water also causes bullets to change course. I can not say that I have seen anyone successfully shoot a fish.

There are fish-tongs, fish-clamps, and fish-rakes. The fish being tonged, clamped or raked are actually shellfish. Shellfish do not count as fish, in my book.

There are fish-traps and fish-shelters, like tubes, baskets, pots, and fences. The Shasta built barriers to drive the fish into traps. Rock fences guided fish into pots and baskets, or into areas where they could be speared or netted.

Nets can be used to catch fish. Some folks scoop. Some catch the fish as they jump. Some folks dredge. Some trawl. Some seine. Some cast their nets. Some just leave the nets in place, hoping fish will get entangled.

Most of these methods are for surface or shallow water where the fish are usually visible. For deeper waters, angling was invented. Angling refers to the use of line, hook and, usually, pole. The fishhook was invented somewhere in northeastern Asia. It was perfected in Japan. The fishhook allowed the Japanese to better adapt themselves to the oceanic aspect of their economy; they could catch fish below the surface. The hook migrated to the North Pacific and then south to Polynesia.

Along with the hook came the use of baits, lures, or other attractants, and the possibility of making fishing a sport or recreation. By that, I refer to one of the unspoken facts of fishing: we choose to make our technique the most difficult for actually catching fish. Anglers rely on luck.

The center of fishing as a sport is luck. As early as the 2nd and 3rd century in Japan, luck was recognized as part of angling with hook and line. The Japanese god of fishing, Ebisu, is also the god of luck and hope. The presence of fish, created out of nothing, their sudden appearance, makes for the moment all fishermen wait for: the moment of startled hope. Hope is at the heart of all fishing.

By definition wilderness is untrammeled by man, so it may seem odd to describe the Russian Wilderness area through its human history. However, history has shaped this area as much as any other force. In fact, events in history provided this wilderness with its name.

The Great Spirit and his family lived on Mount Shasta. Once, one of the daughters was taken off by Grizzly Bear; they were married and their offspring were humans. The grizzly was punished. He was made to walk on all fours and lost the power of speech. The humans were sent off into the world, forced to live an existence half-spiritual and half-wild animal.

This story was told by the first humans to visit what is now the Russian Wilderness Area. The "Shasta Indians" is a name given to four tribes that lived in the Klamath Province. Their culture was a blend of Central Californian, Great Basin, and Pacific Coastal traits.

The Iruaitsu (literally, *people of the valley)*, or the Scott River tribe of the Shasta, used the Russians as a summer camp and food source. Deer, acorns, roots, plants, and fish were gathered. Little is left of their presence, although I have found an occasional broken obsidian arrowhead. Few of their place names are still used. One exception is the county name, Siskiyou, which refers to "council ground," the meeting place of the Shasta, Rogue River, and Klamath tribes.

Fish were the most important cultural resource for the Shasta Indians. Before mining ravaged the Scott River watershed, salmon, steelhead and rainbow trout were abundant. The tribe's most productive method for catching fish was traps and weirs in combination with spears, clubs, and nets. They did occasionally employ hook and line.

Their hooks were made of wood, steamed and shaped, with a barb lashed on. Line was made of cedar bark, or from kelp traded from Indians on the coast. They used small rocks as sinkers. Sometimes, instead of hooking the fish, the Shasta employed the use of wooden lures, attracting the fish to nets, spears, or clubs. Some of these hooks and lures were decorated with carvings and were considered supernaturally potent or spiritually powerful. Fishing was one way of many in which the Shasta entered the sacred aspect of the external world.

The world was considered a dangerous place. Fishing, even though it was a common activity for the Shasta, was considered a going out beyond the known and the safe, and this required magical help. Decorations and symbols carved into their hooks and lures mitigated the dangers. They were necessary to make the passage into the sacred a successful and safe one. The hook and lure demonstrate how the Shasta blended their technology with their religion. They were potent charms.

As a fly fisherman, I know that sense of passage into the spiritual. I, too, feel the need for magic in order to be successful.

The first Whites to pass through the Russian Wilderness Area were Hudson Bay Company explorers. In the 1820s and 1830s, they trapped beavers out of the Scott River. They also introduced diseases to the native populations. Several villages were ravaged by smallpox. In 1850, there were approximately 2000 Scott Valley Shasta tribe members, alone. In 1900, only 40 Shasta, from all four tribes, remained.

Mining attracted the first permanent settlers. Gold was discovered in Siskiyou County in 1850; there were strikes at Forks of Salmon, Scott Bar, Greenhorn, and Yreka Flats. These were mostly placer mines. Later, quartz veins were discovered and shafts sunk into mountain-sides.

Soon after the gold discoveries, Indian slavery was institutionalized. Native Americans were declared "vagabond" by the state legislature; tribal members were sold as laborers to the highest bidder.

Callahan was founded in 1851. French Flat, Springtown, Gasburg, Etna, Black Bear, and Russianville were other camps set up along river banks for the purpose of mining gold. The last, Russianville, was a camp on the Little North Fork and North Fork of the Salmon River. It was this camp and these miners, Russian immigrants, that provided the Russian Wilderness Area with its present-day name.

Also in 1851, in November, a treaty was signed with the Shasta tribe. This treaty was one of many never ratified by the United States Congress, and the reservation agreed upon never materialized. According to Shasta oral tradition, a "celebration" was held for all male members of the tribe. 3000 warriors attended the feast. They were fed strychnine-laced beef and bread. A Yreka newspaper editorialized: "Let our motto be extermination."

In 1852, Siskiyou County was established. Fort Jones was built the same year as an army camp to protect White settlers. The Shasta joined the Rogue River Wars of 1855-6, and, when defeated, tribal members were placed on reservations along the coast of Oregon.

In 1886, the Southern Pacific Railroad was given its land grant and the current checkerboard pattern of land ownership was created. The mines played out. Cattle ranching and timber became the main industries.

Originally, timber had been cut to supply mines and mining towns. In 1905, when the United States Forest Service was established, the Klamath National Forest was created. The Klamath has always been among the most productive forests in the nation, as far as timber harvest is concerned.

Logging was characterized by continuous large-scale production from successive areas of virgin timber. 200 million board feet were cut annually. In 1915 a county booster boasted that "50 billion feet remain to be cut."

In 1933 and 1934, the High CCC Road was constructed on the east slope of the Russians. Heavy cutting ensued and by the end of the 1930s studies predicted "periodic closures of long-established plants" and a "loss of tax base and payrolls" as the "endless" supply of timber started to be depleted. Trees were being cut at twice the growth rate.

Logging continued. The east slope of the Russians was logged intensively in the 1950s, and then heaviest in the 1980s. 200 million board feet was cut annually from 1979 to 1989.

Today, with a depleted supply and rigorous management restrictions, logging has been reduced to a third of its historical levels. If the current management plan is implemented, cuts will be reduced to 60 million board feet. Three-fourths of the forest is reserved from timber harvest due to areas set aside to preserve spotted owl habitat and to protect riparian habitat. Clear-cutting has been eliminated. A large portion of the timbering is already undertaken by helicopters. The forestlands still available for timber management have been put on 180-year rotations.

This area of Siskiyou County is now quiet: dominated by ranches, retirement homes, and a growing tourist economy.

I tried to fish the North Fork of the Salmon earlier today. There were some nice seams in the current down by the bridge, but I could not reach them. A screen of alders, ten to twenty-foot tall trees, grew between me and the flow that might float my flies to some fish. I tried to wade out past them, but as soon as the cold water went over my waist and I began to feel the power of the river's pull, I got scared.

The water was deep between me and the rocky bar where the alders grew. I did not know how deep, I did not know if I could reach the bar; I did not know if I could stand on the slippery stones if I could reach it. I knew how deep the water was in the channel beyond the trees: too deep. So, I got scared and I did not fish, really, and soon joined She'ifa who had been watching from the sandy bluff away from the water.

This was my first time wading since early May, when I almost drowned in my homewaters of Little River. Little River is a coastal estuarine stream where I fish it: with long straight reaches and quiet bends, with dark pools and a few splashing rushes. Fog often whispers in the alders and willows, and rain prickles and dimples the water's surface all winter long. There are cows along the bank. There are marsh hawks and herons. There are otters. The grass and leaves sparkle with dew under the pines and fir; the place is heavy with shadow and gray light. There is always something new to see and hear, always lots to learn from the river. Little River is another intact and ongoing piece of Creation. In places of beauty like that, the catching sometimes lags, but the fishing is always great.

I fish Little River for steelhead, though I never really cared for it. I caught a few, even when I was not very good. I lost a lot more than I caught in the willows that dip their roots and branches into the river, where at low-tide the place resembles a mangrove swamp.

I fish for steelhead mostly to establish myself as an eccentric. You see, when you stand outside in the worst kind of weather, not just stand outside but *in a river* that is cold and dirty, with your mouth tasting like pennies, casting for hours into water that may or may not contain fish (and statistics show that it probably does not) – well, that kind of behavior gives you excuses to behave strangely the rest of the time, too.

Some people fish to widen their boundaries. They fish big water, make long casts. Most steelhead fishermen are like that. I used to be like that. But now, I fish mostly to know my limits. I fish small water, for small fish. I fish tarns in the mountains for little brook trout, or pocket water in rivers for rainbows. I will fish Little River in the late summer for steelhead and salmon smolts. It is fun and lively and keeps my casting in shape.

In early May, wading Little River, I tried to find out its new bottom. Every year the high winter waters carve new channels. By late spring and summer, the water darkens and it is impossible to see the bottom. I like to discover early where I can, and cannot, wade, when the water is still clear. But early May was too soon. The water was deeper than I expected and the sandbar at the ocean must have broken because the river was moving fast.

Most places, Little River is only a few feet deep, but near the banks and around submerged tree trunks and other obstacles, the water digs deep pools. Deeper than a man can stand.

I had made my way down past the farmer's wooden bridge, past the cattle crossing, down the long shallow straights, around the deep pool where all my steelhead had been caught, and I entered the last straight before the freeway bridge. This is where the channel is always trickiest.

With a bottom that is mostly sand, the depth can range from a foot to ten feet. It seems to change from shallow to deep with every footstep and the deeps seem to change location often.

I never learned to swim. I joke now that I never wanted to be a surface lure, but the weightlessness a human being experiences in water nauseates me. Physically, this problem has something to do with my inner ear, and why I am always saying *what?*

There is something beautiful about gravity and its impact on water. The grace of moving water is one of the attractions of fishing. When I am *in* water, however, I lose my sense of gravity. I have learned to be very careful.

I continued wading toward the freeway bridge. The pull of current increased and the water gradually deepened. Before I knew it, I was being pushed. The current lifted me. My feet had no grasp in the sand beneath me and then I felt no sand at all. I was off my feet in deep water; Little River was at my throat.

I could have drowned. I accepted that. Afterwards, after my feet found a foothold, as I walked through the pasture by the nervous cows, as I crossed the river again to make it back to the farmer's bridge and my customary takeout, all I felt was *cold.* I knew the wilderness played for keeps, but it had never played with me before. I knew that fishing was a serious act because lives are always at stake, but, again, it had never been *my* life. I knew that fishing made me part of a very complex situation that involved survival, but *my* survival had never been questioned. Fishing had caught me, I knew that, and the hook is barbed, I knew that, but I never wanted to die for this passion of mine.

Now, in June, waiting to hike into the wilderness, I want to relearn my love for water and fishing. I want to re-experience that conversion when the water takes whatever I give it – polished metal, feather and fur, lifeless eggs or their imitation, a drowned worm – and changes it into something *alive*. I want to remember that the message of the water, even when it is still in a mountain tarn, especially when it is moving, falling, is not so much gravity as it is *renewal*. I want to look at water, reflecting, and imagine it to be a still glossy window into eternity. I want to see a fish shatter that window, and close it tight to bring me back to the here and now.

I am resigned to the present. Sometimes something reminds me of the years, however many, that have made up my life, and then something else tells me to get on with the rest of it. My life. Life is brief and urgent. It is too short for despair. I want to fish again without fear. I want to become part of this world again, part of some place, and I think that fishing is the way to gain access again.

At this campground on the Salmon, She'ifa and I can hear the creek murmur loudly. The water pounds the obedient rocks and continues to flow in a fatal repetitiousness. Deep pools are grooved by the wind to look like the breast feathers of a bird in flight. Alder leaves float like green skiffs. The sky is the sky to a fault. I find that good, to my liking; I want the landscape as it is, and not a mere reflection of my mood.

The wind stirs up the leaves, incites a riot and our campsite resembles an unkempt heap of green birds. A brief rain starts. The campground is stony, sandy, hardened earth. In my pockets, in my shoes and socks and ears and mouth, there is dirt. I take a drink and think nature is superfluous. I know the dirt of the earth without having to taste it. I know the shape of the water without need for the presence of fish. I know there is air without the invention of birds. I wonder if birds hear the air rush through their feathers. I wonder if the world desires human mouths to praise its beauty. I wonder if our words are good enough to describe this creation. I wonder if the unspoken knowledge of beauty is sufficient.

As the wind blows, a liquid quality of light is added to the sky. The air itself becomes a distorting lens. The light is a waving contraction furnished with the obsidian wings of a woodpecker. There is a sweet and sour smell after the brief rain; the whole world smells of wetness. She'ifa and I eat our dinner and prepare for sleep.

During the night, I wake up after dreaming of reading the newspaper again. She'ifa sleeps soundly beside me. Lately, too often, I spend entire nights turning newsprint in my brain. One article detailed how the world was heating up due to the human production of carbon dioxide and other gasses that accumulate in the atmosphere and hold solar heat close to the earth, and how zooplankton, the biological foundation of marine ecosystems, has decreased by 80 percent since the 1950s due to increased water temperatures.

Every page brings another "famine" article; photographs painfully depict how populations grow faster than food supplies. Conservative editorials grumble about developing nations and their inability to control growth. Bleeding-hearts cry for charity. There are comparisons: one additional baby born in the United States consumes as much food and energy as 900 Burundi babies.

I read how it does not "pay" to be a woman anywhere in the world. I worry about She'ifa growing up female. Even at school in this country, still, girls fare poorly, are treated unfairly. They are invisible, absent, quiet. Mostly they do not raise their hands because they are afraid of being wrong; when their hands do go up, they are not called upon. When they speak, they speak quietly, uncertain. After awhile, they disappear. Some keep their hands in their laps now from the fear of being right. It is not just their presence that goes invisible; their self-esteem vanishes as well.

Some writers assert that accumulation of wealth is the answer to all the world's problems, but in wealthy nations like the United States, statistics show that our citizens are better off in almost every measure but one: we are not happier.

We spend more money than ever to educate our students but they learn less. In many schools, the students are smarter than the teachers. Income is twice what it was when I was born, but who feels twice as good? Many feel worse off. In some respects we seem to be *victims* of affluence: mental illness, heart disease, obesity, addiction, battering . . . We seek security in luxury, but we have become spiritually exhausted. We are washed, but not clean. We are victims of hubris: the more we assert our power, the more powerless we become. But still, it seems, we would rather be in power than in love. We would rather consume and acquire than to behold and inquire. The world of wealth seems to promise everything, every titillating sensation and experience, every luxury and comfort, but as individuals we still feel small and maybe even personally diminished

Some writers seem to have rediscovered the second law of thermodynamics and tout its prediction of entropic doom as irrefutable evidence that life is futile. Others describe subtle forms of psychoses that demonstrate that humans are literally losing their grip on reality. It is hard to keep my mind on only one disaster at a time; every page holds another distraction, another option to sink into the quagmire.

Predictions for the future abound. Some speak of an extended status quo. Some write as if *that* were desirable, but for me it reads like another form of pessimism. Some write in a style of enforced realism that negates any attempt to act and maybe even the desire to act, or the desire to desire altogether. Some write of tremendous disappointments to come. Some write of transformations, both good and bad. The present tyrannizes some writers' imaginations, and projections of the future imprison others. Some writers write as if they cannot even *imagine* that things could be different.

Contemporary civilization, or modernity, is on a collision course with ecological limits, that much is clear. The intellectual foundations of the culture are being challenged. The problems we face cannot be solved with the same level of thought that created them.

Political and economic models are being blamed and promoted at the same time. Those who call themselves "progressives" still espouse the technological fixes of the past. I can see that many of the problems I read about in the newspaper are not problems with modernity itself but are problems caused by a blind faith that technology can do everything.

There are critics of capitalism, even when no other economy exists. There are opponents of rationalism. There are adversaries to humanism. These three tenets of modernity are under constant attack. I wonder if perhaps modernity carries the seeds of its own destruction, holds its own negation . . .

Philosophers and thinkers and politicians pretend to have answers, but their ideas fail gracelessly beside the sheer brutal weight of the facts. The world marches lockstep toward doom.

Pollution continues to render greater portions of the planet inhospitable and inhabitable. PCB and dioxin (TCDD) are reported to be a permanent plague. Nuclear radiation lurks. There appears to be no more room for humans to deposit their waste. Landfills are overfull and no new locations can be found. Skin cancer rates are on the rise. Australian papers daily print an index of ultraviolet exposure caused by the hole in the ozone layer. Animal and plant species are disappearing all over the planet at rates of extinction never before experienced. One article states that the planet could lose one-third of its species within forty years. Another notes that we are driving species to extinction at "1000 to 10,000 times the replacement rate." A professor announces the end of vertebrate evolution due to the industrial activities of humans. The human race has always wanted to be god, myths tell, and now we have the power to make the only known "living planet" lifeless.

People are killing each other in brutal wars with increasing efficiency. People, even children, are killing each other at random. Disaster threatens on every page. Progress appears as a disguise for catastrophe. There are new articles about another energy shortage, and there is a plethora of evidence describing the results of energy consumption. The world is crumbling under its own weight.

Everyday at school, while I vacuum and clean, I imagine students meeting individuated, unjust, and untimely deaths. I imagine Jenny, with her children already dead of immune failures, struggling with skin cancer. I dream that Cecelia, a strong competitive swimmer, drowns in a flood caused by the sudden melting of Greenland's ice sheet. I picture Morgan as a suicide after a life of unemployment, poverty, and homelessness. Many I imagine killed in battles – some in wars, some on the streets of cities. Others, I am certain, will die from sheer hopelessness and general boredom.

While I clean, I watch them in their after-school activities – leading cheers, playing basketball, gossiping, giggling, bursting with un-self-conscious youth – but it is too easy to foresee a dreadful future for each. Last spring, we had fundraisers for two still young graduates. One suffered from an inoperable (and as it turned out, *fatal*) brain tumor and the other from some strange benign growth that required massive hip removal and reconstruction and months of chemical therapy for the non-cancerous tumors. It seems an ill omen for the future.

I worry about my daughter surviving this world. I worry about my daughter entering the world of school. She does not share my ambivalence or hesitance. She is looking forward to school. But I worry. The intentions of schools and teachers are good, but the results are scary. I can remember resisting from the start. I did not want to enter school and had to be forced. At the chain link gate, my mother pushed, my teacher pulled, and I cried. I sat sullen in kindergarten for days.

But I adapted. Looking back, I can see how I changed myself to meet the needs of the group. I was socialized. That I had to lose my self, I still can not quite understand. Why my identity had to be destroyed, my sense of self and being humiliated, my dignity lost – that I cannot forgive. I remember the disparagement and how I learned to lower my self-expectation. I remember the compromises: becoming docile, doing what I was told so often that I did not even need to be told. Later, I remember thinking that I was better than others when I did well, but mostly I remember confusion and fear.

I watched other kids change, too. I have class photos in a drawer at home. In a few short years smiling faces deformed into anger and boredom. Bright eyes became dull. Wild energy was tamed and domesticated.

The goal of public schools is to make everyone average, I guess, to prepare us to lead average lives. They have succeeded admirably. I wonder whether She'ifa will submit to being bored. I wonder if her attention span will be trained to be short. I wonder if she will be like I was at times, striving for academic success rather than really learning, if she will lose her curiosity as she is forced to defend herself, if she will crumble when learning becomes the threat of failure, as what is learned becomes symbols without meaning memorized without sense. Will she submit or will she prevail?

And now it is June. As I lie awake, sweated out of another bad dream, I think how my life does not fit into the narrative I read in the newspaper; it is not part of the story. So I am doing what men and women always do when confronted by a crisis: I am withdrawing. I decided to go to the mountains. I am withdrawing to the wilderness. Not having a pristine wilderness, I chose the Russian. Better a wounded wilderness than none at all. I am going fishing.

Summer clouds fill the night sky with a quick, peaceful power and play out dramas with their unearthly forms. The trees, the river, the soil, the rocks and the sledge of the wind play individual melodies. Moles dig in the wet ground undisturbed. Spiders work at their silver ropes. The sky surges over me and below me the waters frenzy. The wind buzzes like a troop of bees in the trees. I think it might rain again. The smell of pines increases, *deepens,* right before it begins to thunder. As I fall back asleep, I am already thinking about packing for our hike.

II. BEWILDERED:
THE STAKES OF WILDERNESS

Breakfast eaten, packs filled, we are on our way. The day is clear and, more importantly, calm of wind. The road to the trailhead has many deadfallen branches to avoid, and there are no other vehicles parked at the end. A solitary hike is promised

Our walk begins with a simple "trail" sign that has fallen to the ground. We climb steeply for a very short distance on a sunny slope before entering the old growth forest where boot treads are softened by a pine needle bed. She'ifa and I climb over or around many deadfalls. We scramble through several creek beds, both wet and dry.

A soft level trail climbs gradually in cool forest shade. The area is pristine, very green, very beautiful. Oregon grape, twinflower, and pine's prince carpet the forest floor. Yew trees are tagged with silver markers to designate a cancer study area.

At approximately the one-mile point, the trail becomes wet and eroded. Several springs, and one hollow tree stump beside the trail, are filled with mosquito larvae. She'ifa and I tread lightly here to avoid creating a muddy mess for future visitors. Next, a steeper climb through rock and brush takes us into the sun briefly before returning to the forest. We notice the diversity of tree species and the size of some specimens. There are some huge old firs, ponderosas, and sugar pines in here. The trees are very dense and have shaded out most of the undergrowth. Old trees lie on the forest floor rotting, their branches thrust out like the ribs of a giant whale on a rusty beach.

In a meadow, over an hour up the trail, She'ifa spots pitcher plants, also known as cobra lilies. I would not have noticed without her bringing them to my attention. I am surprised to find them in this setting. This is a tremendously fertile glacial valley, probably the most fertile place in the world (if diversity of conifers is the measure). These carnivorous pitchers prefer the poor soil of bogs or seeps in serpentine soil. But I guess they should be taken as a sign of the fragile fullness of this place. I should simply find joy in their presence rather than be consternated by their unexpected-ness.

The pitcher plant is a *phytotelma*, or a "plant pond." The plant is structured to store water. The internal ponds capture prey on which the plant feeds; the water also provides a dynamic, self-contained community of life.

Insects are attracted by nectar, most prevalent near the pitcher plant's mouth. Once a bug enters the mouth, it finds escape difficult. If trapped in the pond, the insect will be digested by the action of bacteria.

The plants are attractive, if somewhat odd in appearance, but their odor is not pleasant. Even scientists studying the plants drop their supposed objectivity when describing the smell of a pitcher plant's liquor. One article I read stated that it was "offensive to a disgusting degree;" another described it as a "foul and putrid odor reminiscent of a garbage dump on a still August afternoon."

Interestingly, some animals actually *live* nearly their entire lives *within* the liquor of a pitcher plant. So, not only do insects die in the pitcher, but others live inside them, feeding off the carrion. Klamath Province pitchers have a wider variety of insects associated with them than do pitchers in other regions. This is further evidence of a primitive but diverse ecology, reflected this time inside a single organism.

The trail continues to climb gradually, enters some more meadows, crosses several creeks before reaching the wilderness boundary sign at the two-mile point. South Russian Creek parallels the trail here and is worth a visit. Sandy-bottomed, granite-lined, crystal clear, this is a good spot for She'ifa to soak her feet in the cool water while the warm sun shines down through greenery and birds call in the distance.

My daughter was born late and unexpected in my life. I was forty, her mother forty-five. Both poets, we named her She'ifa, the feminine for *breath* or *aspiration* in Hebrew. In many languages the word for poetry and breathing is one and the same.

She'ifa has spent a good portion of her life out-of-doors. We took her to the Klamath Province for the first time when she was only four months old, hiking up to Grouse Creek Lake amongst some of the oldest rocks in the world on Scott Mountain. She has always enjoyed the water, and thankfully, she has also always left me enough space to continue to be myself. Right now she senses that I want to fish. After a little water play, she dries her feet and says she will just watch.

This is a good place to fish. The water is fast and clear. I see the shadowy shapes of fish and cannot seem to think of a word that adequately describes the speed at which they disappear. There are a few pools where the fish can not see me for the depth or foam. I manage to hook one, lose a few others.

When I fish, even when the catching is slow, my heart beats the way a fish's tail wags; it feels like a flock of birds about to take flight. I do not trust fishermen who are too serious, too good, because I know that the beating of the heart, the lightness in the chest that I can feel all the way to my throat, that the nervousness that makes me blink, also makes my *brain* blink. When I blink, the fish are gone and I am left with nothing but an adrenaline rush and drool on my idiot smiling lips. So, if somebody catches too many fish, if they are that good, that serious, I figure they must be missing *that* feeling. They are missing the *heart* of fishing. And, it seems, then, that they are not really having that good of a time.

I also believe that limits to knowledge are preferable. I do not know much about trout; they are a mystery to me. That is why I fish for them. I know even less about the insects that my flies are supposed to imitate. What I know is that the presence of trout changes the universe for me. Fishermen who are too good, too successful – I figure they also know too much to have a good time.

She'ifa wants to get back on the trail. After a rocky stretch, we enter a large meadow. The ground is human-sized, measured in literal footsteps. And each footstep carries us thousands of years backwards in time, into a previous abundance, while taking us forward, a leap into a healing future.

Once back in the trees the trail makes its first real climb, a true Russian Wilderness climb, up and up and up on switchbacks out of the trees into the sun of a snow avalanche where aspens glitter in the breeze. The tread is rocky through brush. The view is of the headwaters of the creek, granite spires and ridgelines.

The trail climbs across more creeks, into a snow forest at about three miles. The trees are smaller up here and are different species from the lower elevation sections of the trail. The meadows are smaller and widely spaced. Even the flowers are different.

The trail climbs up and up into the headwaters and around an alder swamp. We follow cairns through the rocks and brush and at three and a half miles cross South Russian Creek and begin to climb a staircase trail beside the creek as it ribbons down from Russian Lake. This area is quite eroded and the trail has been reworked recently; we try to stay on the new bed.

A small nameless lake sits in a basin overlooking the valley. The view is spectacular, but so is the sudden, early afternoon appearance of mosquitoes and biting flies. We have our lunch while on the move.

We walk on, crest the ridge and rest for a brief time at Waterdog Lake. Many hikers are camped on the shore. Others have come down to fish from their spots at Russian Lake. A horse is tethered to a tree. People are fishing the lake but there seem to be few fish present. I do not see any being caught.

These people must have come in from the Deacon Lee trailhead, a shorter route with much less climbing. I protest to She'ifa that these hikers did not "earn" their right to a night in the wilderness. A real visit should climb a watershed from the lowland forests to the alpine headwaters and glacial lakes. Guarded on all sides by wilderness and a half day's hike, such places are usually refuges of solitude and I admit to feeling a little cheated when we encountered the crowd that came in the easy way.

"We climbed all the way to the top and that's the way it should be. This is the way it *will* be. This way will be hard, but we'll manage the burden, don't you think?" I ask her, but she is too busy watching frogs in the lake grass to answer.

We decide to push on. The outlet from Waterdog Lake drops straight down the cliff to the two Lower Russian Lakes. The lakes are visible just 500 feet below.

No one is camped there. Golden Russian Lake is invisible, just around the bluff from this pair of lakes.

A faint path drops down the outlet, then slides over gruss and granite. Using tree trunks and branches for handholds, we descend to a wet meadow above one of the lakes.

The descent takes more than an hour, almost two. At the lake, finally, we set up camp. Even though it is clear, the tent goes up to provide a refuge from the mosquitoes. She'ifa plays inside, promises to stay away from the water if she comes outside. I want to fish. I trust her. I also think she will be asleep before she grows weary of playing.

The Lower Russian Lakes are about two acres in size. The eastern lake is shallow, surrounded by meadows and brush. The western lake is deeper, almost completely surrounded by granite. It is a very pretty place. Both are full of large scrappy brook trout, eager for the hook, and strong fighters. I catch and keep a couple for dinner, but my fishing is short-lived. I lose too many lures when large fish drag my line under logs. I want to keep a good selection for our visit to Golden Russian Lake. Also, the bugs are merciless. And I am very tired after the eight-hour hike.

After dinner I sit down with my journal: *These lakes are a place of dark magic. There is wild water fished by only a handful. There are shadowy conifers along the shore, and lots of granite. Shades of blue and green reflect on the lake's surface. It seems to be a haunted place: a place of waiting silence.*

The moon feeds off the twilight, bathed in the soft alpenglow. Luna is a young-bodied satellite, tonight, leaf cool and limbed with melancholy. Her reflective light makes the darkness visible. The wilderness's granite spires, peak-high as peregrines, some still icebound, seem to sprout out of the breathing night. This meeting of rock and sky is full of violence.

I am surprised at that thought, at that word: *violence*. That is not what I mean to say. That is not what I want to say at all. I know *violence* well, and that is not what I mean. There is the rub. The description I am using is a lie.

Some folks say that my thinking is depressing. They wonder if I am depressed. Some question whether I have sought counseling. No doubt I depress them. No matter, never mind, I say.

I would rather use the term *tragic* to describe my thoughts. My thoughts are the result not only of my unconscious, but also the result of a conscious choosing on my part. My worldview, although I take responsibility for it, is beyond easy explanation. I can, however, explain my choice of the tragic.

Humans, I believe, are many-splintered beings, cursed to an existence that cannot be reduced to less than a unity but that also seemingly cannot be experienced as a unity. That marginality is the root and source of my worldview.

Tragic thought is my attempt to re-unify human experience. My thinking is metaphorical experience: beings are connected through relationships; individuals are made integral and complete; the world is made round and whole. It heals me; it makes meanings for me.

I choose tragedy because such thinking reminds me that there is still caring in this world and that that caring is *mine* (or can be made mine if I appropriate it). If I can imagine tragedy, then feelings have not yet been banned. I have faith in the tragic; it is a myth that can bind, a myth with which to confront the often brutal disagreeableness of the truth.

I hear crickets in the grass blades that manage a meager existence in the granite boulders beside Lower Russian Lake. I think, *what is this place?* Crystalline sky strings through the glacial cracks, weaving a shining light through the dark groves of trees. The lake ropes a bent arm around the granite, lacing a stream scent above the naked rock. The pallor of night, black-ceilinged and pocked with stars, knots a mysterious stillness and twines shadows through the small solitude. Wilderness is starting to work on me.

I see many things that gladden my heart but would never be recorded by the reporters from any daily newspaper. Flowers aim their stems for the sun, and bees suck at the pollen-dusted petals. Sunset blossoms in the sky, stars crown the ridgeline. Trees lay dead-fallen from the winter wind. A man, me, is smitten by the untouched beauty of things. Wilderness is starting to work.

I hope that this moment in June is the starting point of a transition, the beginning of a new way of seeing things. I hope that this is the beginning of some kind of healing, some new kind of health.

It is strange, but I am such a solitary person that it takes a trip into the wilderness to make me feel a part of the human community, to make me feel whole. What else is healing and health, if not the sense of wholeness and holiness? Wilderness accomplishes this strange transformation, it leads me out of my suffering in solitude and makes me whole, by simply existing as something, some place, that I have-in-common with others. Having-in-common *is* community.

To have is not the right verb. *To see* is probably better. Vision is a collective activity; possession is too individuated. That someone once saw wilderness as a landscape worthy of preservation because humans did not live there enables me now to rejoin my society. An individual's imagination and perception became the reality; it became a public perception.

Acts of imagination, like the idea of wilderness, are powerfully important. Wilderness is important to me because in a society that has become atomized, made up of alienated persons, the imagination is limited by the range of one's ego. Here, in the wild, *bewildered*, my sense of self is enlarged by a sense of belonging and the imagination reigns powerful again.

This June I have descended into the darkness, cast off into the wild. I am fishing in big waters again, if only metaphorically with my thoughts. I want to transcend the thin trail between cynicism and escape. I want to walk firmly on the earth and be aware of it. I want to be responsive to the possibilities that play might open. Perhaps the awareness of emptiness will inspire some new compassion. I have come to this place to be on a threshold, to gain a new vantage, a perspective of inclusion.

As fatigue overtakes me, I realize my thinking is a lot like this wilderness. Like the plant communities, my thoughts are pieced and patched together. Like the rocks, my thinking is warped and twisted. Like the ridgelines, my ideas are rough outlines. I am bewildered.

The next morning, while She'ifa is still sleeping, I scout the way. The only way out is down, and I know the way will be long. I foresee two hours of steep rocky descent, at least, and another hour of trail-less forest walking up to Golden Russian Lake. Then three hours back to the car on the trail.

When I begin to fix breakfast, a jay, wheedling its brood in a hollow tree, cries out to announce its territory and to denounce our intrusion. This acts as a wake-up call for She'ifa. A thrush calls out in the new morning light. Its voice falls like snowflakes. Then there is a song of silence. When an animal voices itself, a silence always follows. There is an apparent time of moderation, maybe even a time of consideration.

When a human speaks, when even one word is said, there is no following silence, rather a rush is heard. The whole world rushes in. Or, I should say, a whole worldview rushes in. And there is the rub. You see, language is metaphysics and I am coming to believe that the metaphysical core of my modern world is rotten. The results are obvious, already stated, read everyday in the newspaper. This belief is the cause of my renewed despair as I start to break up camp.

Pollen dust filters through the air like a green smoke. The greed of procreation is everywhere. Berries boast of their wasteful arrogance and suffocate the air with scent. Summer is finally hurling into the world and my senses are dizzied. Standing on the granite bluffs, I reel from the beauty. At the lake edge, yellow jackets are drunk on the rotting corpse of a snowbound rodent.

Our first descent is hard going, mostly on sheer rock. In addition to my big pack, I am carrying She'ifa's small bag. For her first overnighter, and being so young and small, I thought it best if she carried little. A change of clothes, a water bottle, and a blanket are in what will become her book bag once school starts.

I scout out small water gullies where grass provides an occasional foot- or handhold. We rest at a small nameless pond on a narrow level shelf. The bugs are merciless again this morning. We discover a crack in the rock that leads the rest of the way down. It is slow going, but unencumbered by her small pack, She'ifa feels confident in her balance. Once in the trees, we follow deer tracks down the forested slope toward South Russian Creek.

While resting beside the water of the creek in a sunny meadow full of corn lilies, I glimpse the quick dart of several smallish trout. I cannot get a good look, but I am sure I see parr marks on these adult fish. Golden trout!

The descent, while slow and stressful, went quicker than I anticipated. Now, She'ifa wants to play. The water here is shallow and sun-warmed; I let her wade by herself if she promises to keep in sight. I need to repack; something is digging into my ribcage. The weight in my pack needs redistributed, a change in arrangement.

I am sensing a change in me as well. The wilderness is doing its work. For one, the wilderness is allowing me to see my despair more clearly. I am starting to see that despair is not the end of the world. Because despair brings with it the possibility of overcoming, of breaking the inexorability of fate, it is really a starting point.

While rearranging my pack, I take out my fly rod and assemble it. Fishing, especially failures while fishing, has taught me about despair and how it can destroy everything I take for granted. There comes a time in the career of every recreational fisherman when nothing that is supposed to work actually works. Say I show up at the river one morning. The air and water temperatures look great; it is the right time of year; I have a good selection of flies that can match any hatch that comes off the water.

But no hatch occurs. What do I do? I despair, because I am a dry fly fisher. I cast a few flies in what I know is a pathetic waste of time. Then I drive home and blame it on the "conditions."

But sometimes I use my despair as a starting point to examine the situation. I abandon my taken for granted expectations and take a look at the unexpected opportunities. Here is an example: I look around, see a bait fisher casting worms into the river and filling a bucket with many more than the limit of hatchery trout. So, I decide to go nymphing and improvise to sink a floating line. Out of my fly box comes a fly that sinks; something I never employ. I learn a new fly fishing skill and catch some fish and go home happy. What happens is I use my disappointment as an excuse to start over. I see the world in a new way. I see myself in a new way. I learn to be happy with what is there.

Learning to be happy with what is there, deciding to leave certain places alone in their undeveloped state, was the impetus behind the Wilderness Act of 1964. The Russian Wilderness Area was set aside by Congress in 1984, recognizing the *legal* definition of wilderness as it applied to this landscape. The different standpoints and perspectives surrounding the concept of wilderness are as old and varied as the human relationship with the earth. How various cultures and individuals look at the wilderness is another example of how we create our realities, accomplish our worlds, make our metaphysics.

Humanity is a species that is detached from its habitat; we stand *over against* the world. Distance *is* the human situation. This is not a negative description; the ability to stand over against the world allows us *to enter into a relationship with it*. Through relationship each of us is allowed to become an individual *person*. Place, wild places, and the human personality have always existed side-by-side. The very word *wild* comes from the word *willed.* Humans are self-willed organisms.

Wilderness is literally "a place of wild beasts." It is a place where the world takes form in the shape of wild animals. Wild trout take the shape of something that slip between my fingers; they take all the elements in wild water and transform them into a particular form of consciousness, a particular way of being in the world (and, thankfully for a poor fisherman like myself, trout have formed a not *too* intelligent kind of consciousness).

One of the things that happens when I visit the wilderness, especially when I keep quiet and go fishing, is that I experience myself as a wild animal in a predator/prey relationship. I get to have a true relationship with another animal. When I fish, everything is loaded with meaning.

Humans have always been predators; the earliest occupations were as hunters and fishermen. Wilderness allows me to practice this job again. Once I experience myself as predator, then I can also experience myself as compassionate. I can catch *and release* trout. I can stalk *and photograph* a deer. In these cases, the act of fishing or hunting becomes functionless but still purposeful. I may not acquire meat, but I do have some fun.

When I venture into the wilderness, when I am *bewildered,* when I am alienated from society and confused by the lack of social norms, I am literally out of control. There are no rules to govern behavior. I become a wild beast again.

I need wilderness to keep the wild alive in me. I need unsurveyed mysteries. I need to witness human limits – mine, society's, culture's – transgressed. I need to make myself open like the wilderness in order to acquire understanding. The wilderness, the living world, is the natural domain of what is left of the wild in the human spirit; it is a refuge for the spirit as well as a refuge for wild ecosystems.

When I visit the wilderness, I am enlarged because I learn an awareness of my limits and acknowledge my narrowness. In a thing like a small fish, I see the vastness of the entire Creation.

The Russian Wilderness Area is a sanctuary and a refuge, but it is not entirely hospitable. By definition wilderness is uninhabited, and should be essentially uninhabitable. It is a place to wander. In most religious traditions the wilderness is a place for a person "to be made ready." In solitude and dread, prophets inflamed themselves toward ecstasy, sought the way without end, and acted as if there was no end.

My sense of wonder is entertained to a large extent by the mystery of nature. Without the beauty of mysteries beyond itself, my mind is deprived of its bearings. A wilderness is a place where I discover where I stand. It is a standpoint.

Place, especially wild places, have been involved in every act of human hallowing. There is no place that is not holy at all times; all that is needed to recognize this is to put off the habitual (literally, that which makes the world dim) – to take off my shoes, so to speak, or to put on my hiking boots. Truth is close to the earth; I have to stoop to find it. And when I find it, there is a wonderful shudder of apprehension as I experience power beyond the self. At least, that is the way the wilderness works on me most of the time.

The human view of wilderness has changed and varied. My modern description of the wilderness and the way it works on me would sound strange to the early Christians. They feared the wild and believed it was cursed. It was a place of exile, where pioneers faced a threat, where they were challenged, and often overwhelmed by the challenge, by the commandment to subdue. To others, however, the wilderness has been a place of sanctification, of purification, a place to seek out divinity because in the wilderness the divine is felt to be near. To all peoples, wilderness gives meaning, however different, to life. To all peoples, the wilderness is a challenge.

Wilderness is important because it exists as the real earth, as an example of the flow of life, as evidence of evolution, as a showing that the wild community still works on humanity. The wilderness is a place of passions, a place that touches my intuitional side, a place where I can relate and connect to the earth in real physical terms and not only through the intellect, not only through abstractions. In the wild, nature embraces me as a part of herself, as within herself. As I feel more and more alienated from the human narrative, spelled out everyday in the newspaper, I need more and more to be embraced by the rough arms of a wild world.

Wilderness satisfies human needs that cities and civilization cannot satisfy. I have wild roots, and in these green enclaves that were accidentally left behind, I am reminded of these roots and experience them again. Even in a wounded wilderness, like the Russian Wilderness, I become aware, and awareness implies responsibility. For example, here I see a self-healing world that, if left alone for 100 years, will gradually re-establish an original state of ecological equilibrium. The trick, of course, is to experience and enjoy the wilderness in such a way that leaves it alone. I tread lightly, pack a stove instead of burning wood, carry out all my garbage . . .

One of the experiences with which the wilderness constantly challenges visitors is that of uncertainty. Weather is unpredictable; geology is unstable. Trees fall to block the path; whole mountainsides slide to remove a trail or road.

Human existence, too, is uncertain; we are a species that will never *be* because we are always *becoming.* Our existence, our *being,* implies being vulnerable. There is no grace or gift in human life; what we have and what we are must constantly be won.

We live in a *changing* world. I see that in the wilderness just as I read about those changes everyday in the newspaper. But it is not an irrevocably *changed* world, and the process of change is not independent of our will. The future depends upon us, upon none other than ourselves.

Again, I think, despair can be a starting point.

Despair, as I define it, is living with full awareness in the face of uncertainty. Despair is a confrontation with the world, a confrontation centered in insecurity, a trying for the best possibilities of the moment. To recognize or admit uncertainty and darkness as a condition of life – that is a start. The best is a limit. And what is wrong with *enough*?

Here in the meadow, early summer has taken hard hold today. When the breeze is just right, I hear the grass crackle as it begins to dry. I smell dust steaming.

The shadows are longer in the forest today as well. The animal trails we have followed are dustier, too. The sun finally crests the spine of the wilderness and cascades in shafts through the dense needling of the forest. Near the creek a slight wind has picked up and the alders blow like flames. The summer light sparkles in the paling leaves and emboldens small cones to set seeds. The leaves are wet, and as I creep beneath branches to reach the water to fish, they wipe against my face, mix with my scent, begin to wither, blend into the wholeness that I always sense in a wilderness.

III. FISHING AND THE METAPHYSICS OF GRAMMAR

Out of the meadow, the brush is thick and difficult to negotiate, especially with a pole. She'ifa's hair is getting caught in the branches, too. She is getting frustrated. I try to distract her by pointing out some birds. The birds have it easier than She'ifa and I. They fly free in the clean air, find shade and cool winds; we plod through brush in the mid-morning heat.

The earth has many mouths, many voices. Today, grasshopper's crackling fireworks tell the tale. The noisy presence of all these "terrestrials" makes me glad: easy bait to catch some golden trout. The bait might be easy to catch, I remind myself, but catching a fish is always a matter of chance.

Fishing has taught me about uncertainty. First, there is the uncertainty of the water itself. When I cast into the unseen depths of still water, I cast into mystery. I fish blind, presenting my lure or fly to likely spots. At many lakes I fish, I am not even certain what I might catch (let alone if I might catch anything at all). Moving water offers yet another contact with mystery and uncertainty; water in motion offers a view of the continuity and permanence of the universe. The water keeps on flowing without end, but the constant change in a river's flow also shows that the universe is full of possibility.

Second, there is the uncertainty of the fish. I never know what a fish will do. Odd things happen. Fishing is a confrontation with something beyond my knowledge, a way of contacting with mysteries. I am still learning, always learning. I do not know much about trout life cycles and even less about the lives of the insects my flies are supposed to imitate. I have never figured out what my lures are supposed to represent to a trout. I am stupefied by all the choices in rod, reel, line, and hook that a plethora of catalogs offer me several times a year. I do not know that much about water. I cannot "read" it like some experts. Once, for example, I mistook a patch of water weed for a rock and spent the rest of the day in wet jeans.

I probably would be a better fisherman if I learned more about fish, about their feeding habits, about the lives of the things they feed on, and about the equipment I use. Even with that knowledge, I still would not know what it is like to be a fish. That is the way I like it to be. When I am fishing I know that I do not know what is going to happen. That is one of the reasons I fish: to be in a state of alert receptiveness.

Fishing in a state of receptiveness has shown me that all things are connected in functioning relationships. If I want to understand the truth of any one thing, I have to allow that there are no reducible truths; the truth is no less than the whole thing, the whole of the ongoing Creation. This awareness is both an expansion and a limit.

If I recognize my limits, I discover myself. If I rediscover the expansiveness in mystery, I rediscover sources for solace and joy. I trace my thoughts back to their source and, strange enough, I see that despair begets hope – because of its uncertainty, even. Despair can be the basis on which to build a consolation. Despair *is* the starting point.

The articles I read in the newspaper spread the word that this is a time of dread. Dread is a special kind of despair because, like tragedy, it reveals caring. Dread is the point where caring breaks through to force attention on the things that went unnoticed. Dread causes me to *be careful*. I am enabled to re-learn the things I truly *care for*.

The coast where I live is littered with shipwrecks. The mountains She'ifa and I hike in are laced with piles of storm damage. I reject the doom that a wracked landscape seems to inspire. Instead, I am learning to value my choices. The entire world depends upon individual choices; my world is identical to the stuff from which my choices are made. No one else can make my world. *I am all there is.*

Part of me is not saddened by the news reports of a coming era of ultimate challenge to civilization. I hope we will finally be shocked to ask and find the answers to problems. I am more than certain that many, if not most, of our problems, the sources of the despair I feel after reading the newspaper, can only be solved morally, by changing our values. Life must be moralized; ethics must become part of the passion of life.

Change requires *shock.* Metaphysical, ontological, and epistemological roots need to be shaken to their core before action will occur. *Am I going to accept despair without doing anything?* What I hope, why I see despair as a starting point, is that maybe crises, times when observations no longer fit expectations, can shock me into action, can help me retool my mind.

Crises signify that it is time to change, a signal that change is absolutely needed. Crises force radical selections, bold choices. Crisis, like despair and dread, results in self-awareness. I hope crises can clear my mind to make better choices.

Maybe the prospect of crises can even help reveal the absurd, and help me to understand absurdity. This is not to say that I believe the universe is absurd, but rather that my *experience* of the universe is absurd. Absurdity arises when reality contradicts my expectations; things are not what I would have them be. But absurdity, too, can be another starting point. As a perspective, as a standpoint, absurdity allows me to challenge the conclusions of reason and logic. Absurdity reveals that such conclusions are irrational and illogical. Once again, I find myself in a position to start over. The world is re-newed, vital, full of life, and I am part of it.

I need to rediscover what the world is for, and who I am within it. I need to choose my relationship with the earth, and the language I will conduct that relationship in. In short, what I need to do is to re-construct my reality, my worldview. I have to move, I have to change my perspective. I need a new anchorhold.

Fishing has taught me about standing places, too. Once, on a steelhead expedition, I grew bored and upset with not finding fish in what seemed a barren Redwood Creek. I started to fish for the small smolts I saw in a calm backwater. A man walked upstream and waited patiently for me to move from where I cast single salmon eggs to the immature fish. Then he cast a plug precisely where I had been standing. He hooked and landed a sixteen-inch steelhead. He caught this fish out of my literal footsteps. Changing my standpoint can alter my whole perspective on the world.

By changing my standpoint, I see more clearly. It is not the way things are that depresses me, but rather it is the way I have chosen to see how things are and how I have chosen to describe the way things are.

I have accepted a deficient code for reading the world. Crises breed in my worldview. Crises breed in my head. That *is* depressing. It is also a hopeful theory. Take greed, for example; greed is mental. Greed can only be satisfied mentally, not by consuming the things I think I desire. Most of the crises I see are likewise mental. Which means they can be solved mentally: change my view, change my perspective, change my standpoint, change my description, and the gate to satisfaction, happiness, and contentment is opened wide.

Despair is the starting point. The thought becomes a chanted mantra.

How do I start over? From a standpoint of Idealism, *no*. From Rationalism, *no*. From Transcendentalism, *no*. I found within the existing human situation the sources of my despair. I came to realize that despair has created absurdity, me as an absurd *person.* As a person, I can relate. Relationship creates new involvements, new social systems, and new moralities in the world. For me, despair has exposed a new way of talking: the choice to find a language that suits the world.

Despair *is* the starting point. I find myself at a crossroads. I see how my language has transformed itself into arrogance and destruction. It is time to dispense with arrogant words (and the attitudes behind them); it is time to find a language that is humble. This is not just a semantic task; it is a moral quest. If I surrender my arrogance and regain the true confidence of humility, maybe I can reclaim my true humanity.

Life was given to me as an empty space, as an open problem, as a task. A starting point, then, is to fill life, to *occupy* it with my choices. Too often my life is occupied with habits, with routine drudgery, with work: three more inventions of modernity. Work has become the modern occupation.

One of the first human occupations, from time immemorial, was that of *fisherman*. There are still people who fish for a living, still people who try to make money by fishing. They want to be a part of the economy, as fishermen. On that scale, in those terms, fishing is a small occupation.

A few years ago, I decided that I wanted to become a fisher. I chose to occupy my life with a dedicated pursuit of fish. When I chose to occupy my life with fishing, I was not talking about becoming a part of the gross domestic product (although the purchase price of licenses, gear, clothing – all the accoutrements of the sport fisherman – have become a large part of my budget and probably account for my biggest donation to the economy). I was talking about the moral pursuit of fish as a sport, as a re-creation. I was talking about choosing to occupy my space here on earth as a person who tries to deceive trout with a fly or lure. This is the character I want to become in the narrative of the world. This is the plot I am choosing for my existence.

There are certainly easier things to do. I spend a lot of money and time and effort to put a trout back where it came from, back where it belongs.

Part of catch-and-release fly-fishing's joy is this "purposeful uselessness" and unreasonable-ness. I handicap myself by choosing rare prey, trout. I handicap myself further with my techniques for catching. It would be far easier and more effective to build a weir, use a gillnet or even a club, but I usually insist on using dry flies with barbless hooks. Dry flies are designed to work rarely, only when insects are hatching or dying on the surface. When I choose to fish with lures, there will be days when fish will eat nothing below the surface because they are gorging on the hatching or mating or dying insects on the surface. For me, however, this state of affairs is just what I want. I want something I can do, some place where I can go, where rationality is limited if not excluded.

I choose to make fishing a hardship, but that too is the point. Hardship requires effort, concentration, and a quality of attention. These are my real goals while fishing. What I want is a certain attitude towards the world. I want to really be *in* the world. When I fish, I am *in* the world, my mind is on the environment, I am an alert participant.

I want to occupy a space where the waters are alive with chance. I want to be a human being as an animal again. I want to return to the primitive, to the unchanged, to nature, to a place where occupation means a place to stand. A standpoint. An anchorhold.

From our standpoint, She'ifa and I cannot see where we are going. South Russian Creek drops straight and steep on its course. We descend a game trail, steadily. The trees part and the view of the granite headwall expands. The sun continues to cycle through the sky. It is late morning and I am not at all aware of where we are. The trees close in again, standing tall in protective folds.

The trail crosses a scree of granite, tumbled from the cliffs above. Late morning sun floods the forested slopes to the west. The trail flattens, emerges into a meadow of bear lily that borders the now placid creek.

A large wet brushy area surrounds the meeting place of the outlets from the Lower Russian Lakes and the outlet from Golden Russian. She'ifa and I avoid this swamp by staying close to the rock on the south and then crossing the Golden Russian outlet. We keep the creek to our left and get into the trees for easier going. The trail starts to climb, then gets steep, rocky, with aspen and alder providing some obstacles. We cross the creek, follow a clear trail up and through the steep rocks to a shelf.

Surely, we are not the first to walk these trails. Others have come before us. Fishermen and backpackers have followed the deer tracks through the pine needles. I would like to think that the original inhabitants of this land, the Shasta, wandered through here, as well, in search of game and to fish.

In the early days, South Russian Creek teemed with salmon and trout; deer, bear and other game were abundant in these mountains; the meadows provided many vegetable foods; and, at lower elevations acorns were in large supply. The Russian Mountains and the Scott River Valley were ideal sites for a hunter-gatherer community.

Modern anthropologists believe that the Shasta, together with other Hokan language speaking tribes like the Karuk, Yana, and Pomo, were part of a band of Indians that crossed the Bering Strait 10,000 years ago to become the original settlers of California. The Shasta, on the other hand, believe they were created where they lived, right here where She'ifa and I hike.

In spring, when specific plants grew to a certain height, the Shasta abandoned their winter villages along the river and moved to the mountains where they lived for the summer in open roofless brush shelters. They collected and ate pine and hazel nuts. There were berries: manzanita, blackberries, serviceberries, elderberries, gooseberries, thimbleberries, chokecherries, and sumac. They had milkweed for chewing gum. They ate roots, bulbs, and seeds from the meadows. There were deer, elk, sheep, antelope, bear, mountain lions, bobcats, rabbits, squirrels, birds and insects for meat. There were salmon, trout, suckers, eels, crawfish, and turtles to be caught. Rather than the pole, hook and line that I use, the Shasta dammed rivers with wooden stakes and brush to trap their prey in willow baskets. They also used nets and spears. Theirs was an abundant and varied diet, and all food was shared within the village.

In the fall, after the venison was collected and dried, when the berries were stored in baskets, the people returned to their winter villages on the river. Though the villages were small, life centered around the relationships within them.

The Shasta lived in a territory bounded by mountains: the Marble Mountains lay to the west, Mount Shasta was to the southeast, Red Butte was at the northwest corner of their world and Mount Pitt provided the northeast reference. They accepted this world without trying to explain it. The Shasta believed that their world always existed and that they were created in it. Everything in the world always existed as well; each thing only needed to be named. Theirs was a landscape teeming with the spiritual powers of mystery.

The Shasta spent their entire lives on one small piece of the earth and with one small band of people. By living in one place, they contributed to the continuing harmony of the world. Their lives centered around relationships: with the land, with the family, with the spirits. Because interrelationship was the dominant focus of the culture, ethics were also of prime importance.

The Shasta lived in numerous villages scattered over their terrain, including along the Scott River at the base of the Russian Mountains. The Scott River tribe was known as *Iruaitsu*.

The family was the major social organization within the village. Each village consisted of 30 to 40 people, from two or three families. Estimates for the entire tribe's population range from 2000 to 10,000.

Each family had a dwelling, but within the village there was also a group house, a sweat lodge, and a menstrual hut. The buildings were dug into the ground, perhaps as much as four feet. Short walls made of cedar bark extended above ground. Sugar pine boards made up the roof. The floor was dirt, with a fireplace in the center. Blocks of wood served as stools.

The sweat lodges were dug deeper into the earth and had ladders for access; they were larger and taller versions of the dwelling house. There was usually one lodge per village; it belonged to the headman, but any man who contributed to its construction had rights to use it. Most of the males slept together in the sweat lodge during the winter.

Women remained in the dwelling house with the children, except during their menses when they were segregated into menstrual lodges.

The village would be scattered with obsidian tools, soapstone containers, wooden spoons and bowls, bone knives, fire drills, cords of hemp and root, nets and baskets of hazel, yellow pine, grasses, and ferns. The people wore animal skins, buckskin mostly. The men had buckskin moccasins with elk or bear soles, buckskin leggings that reached from ankle to hip, a breech-clout, and, in cold winters, a shirt. The fur was left on the animal skins for cold weather warmth. Women wore moccasins, a skirt (plain for most days, a dress skirt for dances and other ceremonial occasions), an apron, a shirt, and a cap; these too were mostly made of buckskin, except the cap which was woven, with occasional beadwork.

Both sexes grew their hair long. The men gathered theirs on top of the head with a bone pin; the women used braids. Women were tattooed, usually on the chin. They played games and gambled, had flutes and rattles for music.

The Shasta were a peace-loving people. Each day began with the headman reciting a prayer urging them to be industrious, to do good, to have a kind heart, and to live in peace.

Climbing through this forest with my daughter, it is easy for me to imagine that such a life was possible, and maybe is still possible. Imagining possibilities is another starting point. The Shasta took pleasure in their earth, in the meadow grass and ridge tops, in the curled waves on the river's surface, in the clean views, in the soaring thrust of cedar. And they left us all that. I wonder what we will leave. Iron cables rust in the slashed forest on the eastern slopes of this wilderness. Barbed wire, eroded riverbanks, oil patches on dirt, real estate signs . . . Do we believe this is enough? Is this enough to leave to those who will come after us? Considering the consequences of my behavior, contemplating my legacy – that, too, is a starting point.

She'ifa and I walk on a faintly seen but easily hiked path that leads us through the forest. This is a dark and dense place. The trees are large but grow in thick stands. Little light penetrates the canopy; no brush covers the floor. There is only the thick and soft and sometimes slippery pile of conifer needles that cushions our footsteps.

The climb becomes gradual, again, and the trail veers toward the creek. We hear water falling and running quickly over rock. There is sunlight ahead and a patch of bright, broadleaf greenery. The trail nears the water in mottled light. This fork of South Russian Creek drains Golden Russian Lake. It does not carry a lot of water but here the gradient is steep and gravity pulls the water down with speed. There are many places where the riverbed is solid rock, others where the water drops over six-foot ledges. Green ferns grow in red rock. Lupines grow bright in the thin soil.

We pause for a rest and a snack in the sunlight and watch the morning shadows dance in the shape of leaves. There are birds high in the sky, I cannot tell what kind, but they seem to be circling in a thermal. Although I cannot soar, I sense that my thoughts have taken flight.

The morning breeze keeps the bugs down . . .

I must not have gotten enough sleep last night. I dozed off in the sun. I do not carry a watch so I am not sure how long I napped. The sun is not much higher. She'ifa is still occupied with her crackers. I guess there will be time enough still to reach the lake, fish and make the return hike. Anyway, it was good to exercise my dreams, too.

The trail climbs steeply away from the creek, back into the trees, and then higher into brush and rock on the sunny slope. We parallel the forest below, and when the creek brings the trees back up to us, forest and trail meet in a wet alder marsh. We take the high route to the west. Another animal trail brings us back to the creek, further up. The volume of water is much less here.

The trees thin at the base of a rock face. Water tumbles straight down a slot. Golden Russian Lake must be in the bowl on top of these rocks.

The Shasta, had they come to this part of their world, would have known the way up the rocks. A story would have taught them the directions, maybe even would have gotten into the details of where the foot and handholds were. Stories told all of the tribe's truths and laws.

Individual names were given in terms of story, too. The Shasta did not name their children until they were one or two years old. Usually, children were named after an animal, especially birds, based upon some personal characteristic that was discernible in both the human and their animal totem. The Shasta kept their names life long, not changing them at adulthood like many other tribes. Shamans helped in the naming process.

Shamans helped in nearly every village experience. Shamans, usually women, were persons of great importance because in their ceremonies the whole ritual and experience of the people was included. They were dreamers and doctors, visionaries and storytellers.

Before coming to the wilderness, I read about the place, the history, and the Shasta. I even picked up a little of their language. Now, She'ifa and I ford (*hauna*) the creek (*kinapxig*). The water (*kumma*) is cold and fast and clear, but very shallow. I see a trail (*k'enom*) going up the mountain (*kip*). If we follow it, I bet we will wind up at the lake (*t'in'apxau*) where we can begin fishing for trout (*sa'hawai*). The sound of the Shasta language, if I hear the words right, mimics many of the sounds in their world.

A tunnel of a path leads through some alder brush over mossy stones. There is water under the rocks surfacing in thin runnels. At the base of the rock face proper, in the sun, a clearer path shows itself. A shelf of rock with thin soil and meager grass angles up the face, then doubles back like a switchback to the top.

Halfway up, there is a strong salty smell. Bear, I guess. But my excitement pushes me onward without fear, although the odor has instinctively risen the hairs on the back of my neck – quite a feat when just an instant prior the same hairs were matted to my neck with sweat.

On top, I help She'ifa descend a small wall of rock. We pass through a big meadow of grass and bugs. Campsites are on a bare dirt spot; they look rarely used.

I am anxious to fish. *Let it be for golden trout.* We drop our packs against a tree trunk. She'ifa forages for lunch. I walk around, but still no lake is visible.

There is no room for a lake higher up. I can follow the snowmelt from the ridgeline to this bowl. I stop to rest and think. A few early afternoon clouds are torn to shreds on the peaks to the west. A few more tumble to disappear in the valley above me. A breeze carries the sigh of trees. Small birds float among the branches like pale wraiths. The waft of bear scent, fertile and odorous, fecund and raw, swirls in the grass. I lick the salt from my lips, rest my head against dark shadow-pine bark, dig my feet into the grass, feel rough stones in my hands. Cloud shadows play hide and seek on the mountain ridge. The ridge shoulders the weight of the sky. Sunlight sparkles on a bird's wing. Blossoms crown the wet meadow slopes.

I decide to climb to the water I see tumbling down the granite. I figure I can follow the water down to the lake, or maybe get a view of it from above.

"Well, that's what your life has been like," a Shasta tribe-member might have said of my not exactly being lost in the woods and of my not ever really finding what I am looking for, either. Hopefully, someone will say now, *"Kwam•aka•huk."* (He's on a high place watching). And, then, *"Kwa•m'a•'ik."* (He's fishing with a hook and line).

I follow the rim of rock toward the headwall, but before I reach it I encounter a wet meadow of corn lily and azalea. The leaves and flowers flutter in the wind, head high. There is a slow drain of water following the intricacies of gravitational force. I sense a clearing in this wet growth and head toward it.

Without knowing it, I have found Golden Russian Lake. Shallow and small, set in trees and brush, the lake is difficult to see until I am right next to the shoreline. Grasses, willows, and ferns grow into the lake; the west shore is granite. At 5700 feet, Golden Russian Lake is one of the lowest in the wilderness. It is rapidly filling in, especially on the south end, and is now less than an acre in size, whereas an old DFG anglers' guide states that it was two acres in size.

The lake was stocked with golden trout in the past. Most have crossbred with rainbow trout. The result is a trout that is small, 6 to 8 inches long, and with the coloration of rainbows combining the parr marks of golden trout. In spring and early summer, these fish are in their spawning finery, their coloration is truly beautiful. I hope to see one soon on the end of my line.

Golden Russian Lake is a small body of water, perhaps only slightly larger than a half acre. The water is dark and reflective, a chameleon of color. The lake is shallow on this brushy side; I can see the bottom even in the darkness. On the far "shore," I imagine the water must attain some depth, as granite drops sheer into the lake.

I walk in the water to traverse the shoreline; there are only a few clear areas plus a few rocks to stand on. In places, the bank is sheer, undercut, and the water is deep. I see snails skim the water-film ceiling of the lake. Damsel and dragonflies are engaged in fine-stitch flights, but keep away from the water. Near the perpendicular meeting of stone and water on the far shore, close to what must be the outlet, some small fish break the surface by jumping after insects. I need to get back to my pack and assemble my ultra-light rod. I need to find a way to get She'ifa to the water, and a place for her to stand or sit.

The starting point in fishing is to read the water. I do this now, in my un-expert way, even before I go fetch my rig. I see some small rises on the far shore, where the granite ends and some brush begins. Bugs are probably falling off the leaves into the water and the trout are being opportunistic. There is no hatch or other insect bounty. No fly-fishing here. But lures might work.

I walk back to my pack. She'ifa asks, "Where's the lake?"

I tell her how I stumbled upon it just a few feet from where we now eat lunch. I drink some water, change shirts. After a long anticipation, I guess I am putting off the consummation. I unzip my pack's main compartment and reach for the hard plastic case that contains my ultra-light rod and reel and lures.

The rod assembles quickly. There are five pieces. The reel slides in a sleeve, the sleeve screws tight, the reel's handle also screws in easily once I go through the mental calculations that will give me a right-hand retrieve. The two pound test is virtually invisible in bright light and is difficult with altitude swollen hands to run through the guides, but I manage. I tie on a swivel snap, a very tiny one, clip off the knot end, and look at my selection of lures.

The water is dark and unclear, but the day is bright. The fish are small. I snap on a small brass, dressed lure. I pocket the lure box. She'ifa wraps her legs around my hips, her arms around my neck and I carry her through the brush toward the lake. I find a rock big enough for both of us to stand.

I start casting. I aim, not for the far bank, near the granite and brush where I saw the fish rising, but for the inlet shallows. This is my strange way, another habit in which I handicap myself: I hold out the surest thing for last.

My aim is true and the cast is good – not that it matters, yet. I let the lure free sink before retrieving. I wait, then reel.

When I choose to occupy my life as a serious fisherman, fishing becomes a metaphor for my life. Fishing is how I experience and understand the world. I live to fish and I fish to live. I fish for life and live for fish. The metaphors become real.

My talk and writing about fishing becomes metaphorical as well. Naturally enough, many of the metaphors concern language. Often I describe how I *read* the water, or, treat the water as a text. There is danger in this because the water is not a book. How I use language is of vital importance. It is another starting point and standpoint. How I call things, what I name them, is how and what I see.

When I look at a river or a lake, I want to see water. Words inevitably change water, the river or the lake or the ocean, into something else; words make the water words. This means that I must choose my words carefully because my words are what the water will become. It is part of my human arrogance and dominance to see things only in and on my terms rather than in and on their own terms. It is demeaning and devaluing to change something into what it is not.

One way I can choose my words carefully is to resist the technique of personification. Personification is the representation of a thing as a person or by the human form. It is not a bad thing. The desire behind personification is quite beautiful; the desire is for a relationship. This desire becomes misguided when I think I can only relate to persons and therefore change rivers, trees, rocks, or animals into what they are not in order to relate with them. Instead, I must learn how to relate to the non-human.

I need to learn to speak of the non-human in its own language. I need to learn to speak the language of each individual, specific river or lake. Or tree or rock or animal or mountain.

The water in Golden Russian Lake is dark. I have never fished it before. I cannot see the fish, except for the few rises on the opposite shore. I have heard the rumor of golden trout, but it is just a rumor and fishermen's stories often "don't hold water." Talk is cheap. So, in essence, I am casting to chance.

I fan cast, covering the entire lake. I start at the far end where snowmelt drips into the lake from a wet meadow. I move toward the depths beneath the granite, and finally end up near the brush at the lake's outlet. I get no strikes, see no pursuers, until I reach the spot near the brush. I feel a slight tug. I let She'ifa cast. She has been practicing all spring and is waiting so patiently. Her lure bounces off the granite into the water. She pulls back fast, skipping the lure over the surface, then lets it sink. I remind her to reel. She says she feels something. "Pull back on the pole," I tell her, "Set the hook."

She does. I see a live weight pulling the line askew. It is a small struggle and when the fish nears shore there is some tail-walking and jumping.

The fish is small, maybe seven inches long; I would probably be pushing it to say it weighs a half-pound when wet. The flesh is only knuckle deep. I keep the trout in the water, where it has calmed but still keeps a constant counter pressure on the line. This fish is a cross-breed: rainbow trout mixed with golden trout. This is June, so the full glory of a golden trout's color is present, and the parr marks are unmistakable. The fish has a dark green back with black spots, pale moon-colored sides in which darker parr marks are visible, seemingly embedded deeper in the skin. The belly is nearly yellow. There is some very vivid coloration, when I look closely, that is not rainbow-like. There are purples and oranges and blues in the parr marks, maybe some gold and red. The fish is missing the rainbow's classic mid-body stripe of crimson. It is a very beautiful little fish.

I wet my hands to hold the fish, still in the water, and shake the barbless lure from its lips. The fish swims away, unhurt. She'ifa is smiling, satisfied. She hands the pole to me. I cast for another hour, use every lure in my collection, but I do not catch another one.

She'ifa sits on the rock, lies down, leans her face over the water. Of course, the water reflects her. I realize the water's reflection shows her only because she is calm and still. All is well, I think.

The sun is high and hot now, with no breeze to cool it off. I pack up my rod, put away lunch. We pass the water bottle and start the hike back.

I am no expert and know only one language well, but I do know that language creates a worldview and that different languages create different worldviews. That is the thought that begins to fill my head as we hike back to the trailhead. The deer trails through the forest seem easier this afternoon, or maybe the angle of sun and the angle of descent makes the passage more visible. We pause at the creek to rest. The sound of fast moving water is refreshing.

The final drop is quick and easy. I see a few more of the larger cross-breed trout at the meadow crossing. She'ifa plays in the cold water while I assemble my fly rod and drift flies. Nothing. She'ifa brings me a grasshopper she has caught. I hook it to my fly, drift it, and in the froth below a log, I hook *my* golden trout.

As we head on down the trail, I notice that some of the crossings that were dry yesterday morning are trickling water this afternoon. The trail grinds on and my mind wants to reach some finality about language, to draw conclusions that will somehow relieve the despair that pushed me inland to this wilderness.

My despair is a product of my worldview, and my worldview is a product of my language. The vocabulary of despair is contained within my use of language; how I speak and write and think makes me see the world despairingly.

She'ifa's starting school was one genesis for this trip. The dishonest use of words at public schools is a major concern of mine. Students listen to words that are used in ways that are not true, in ways that may not even be meant. I do not want my daughter to unknowingly participate in the dishonest use of words.

As an example, one of the most frequently used words in public schooling is *appropriate*. It is one of my favorite words, but not in the way schools use it. Administrators refer to "appropriate behavior." Teachers refer to "appropriate methodology." What they both really mean is "acceptable." They use the word "appropriate" as an *adjective* or *adverb*, meaning "compatible" or "fitting." Students should fit in; teachers should conform, teach the standards.

"Appropriate" is a Latin *verb* meaning "to make ones own," or "to possess exclusively." My goal in coming to the wilderness was to appropriate a worldview that might lead to happiness. I hoped She'ifa might come away with an experience that could lend her the strength to remain herself.

Another word that is often misused in school is "comprehension." Comprehension has been misunderstood to mean retention and regurgitation of facts. Schools measure comprehension through the use of standardized tests. This concept does not contain the original meaning and roots of the word. Comprehension is "mind grasping" and "understanding" and "getting it" (as in, to appropriate knowledge, or to make facts ones own).

I often fall back on my training in philosophy when I want to make sense of things. Metaphysics is the realm of philosophical inquiry that studies the human understanding of the nature of the world. I cannot know the real stuff of the universe. I cannot know *that* truth. For me, metaphysics is the study of what I *do* know: that is, the "logos," the account, the language of the universe, the language of being in the universe. Language is reality for me. Language is where I live. Things exist for me, as they are, because I name them. Language is a metaphysic. Language is how I appropriate the world.

What I learned when I studied metaphysics was that my world is unique. The term "the world" really refers to ones unique awareness; the world is ones unique individuated experience of it. As a unique individual, I occupy a place, a physical location; I have a standpoint. Where I stand is a choice; implied is moral responsibility.

There are alternative ways of understanding the world, there are various metaphysics, there are various ways of telling the truth. I am responsible for these choices.

My thoughts are expressed in language. How I speak is how I think. How I think is an expression of my intentional attitude. How I think and speak is how I see. The words create the world. I am responsible for my world. I am responsible for the words I choose and for their consequences. The burden of responsibility, of being held accountable for results, is the starting point from which every perspective results. Perspective is the outcome of the way I see the world which is dependent upon the words I see the world with. Perspective is a standpoint.

She'ifa and I are very much in the same position. We are at a starting point. The world is open and unfinished for both of us. We are not subject to inexorable fate. The very unpredictability of the world, and of our roles within it, can make our journey interesting.

My choice, I realize, as we near the end of the trail, is to continue to try to be happy despite the odds. I have to make a stand, to choose a standpoint, to take a stand, and accept the consequences of it. My choice is my anchorhold.

IV. AFTERWORDS

Hay lies in rows, catches the light and casts shadows; the flats in the Scott River valley look like a huge curving striped flag of earth. The air is full of dust as farm machines scoop and thresh, cut and bale; the land is left in a mere bearded stubble. There is a quality of light, an angle of shadow, a tarnish in the golden glow that hints at the change of season. Summer is in full bloom.

Cattle rest under cottonwoods, oblivious to the cycling. Captured in the still afternoon, the cud-chewing animals look like so many black stones laid out on the bare soil.

And now it is August. Seeds are already sleeping, covered in leaf fall and needle duff and soil dust. It is still a long time before the winter rains will come. The lakes are getting murky with algae and insect detritus and excreta from fish and amphibians. The cloudy water is wrapped up in reeds at the lake edges. It is a high hike up the creeks, a long way up the ridges to where the water might be clear. In Golden Russian Lake, the trout are feeding heavily, knowing that another winter lies ahead.

And now it is August. I take my leave of the wilderness to tell my story. My story does not belong there, in the wild; it belongs out here, in the world.

She'ifa starts school tomorrow. She has readied herself beyond anything I could help with.

I am thinking anew on words, especially on the word *is*. I am thinking that the fate of the world might rest upon how the word *is* is used. For a start, let me from now on speak of a *human bein*g as a verb instead of as a noun. This little change in language could create a perspective of the world that might reveal the possibilities of acting in a world where I make my own future.

She'ifa's future is both a promise and a task. She has an opportunity, like each of us, to take hold of her destiny. She can accept fatalism, say that of hunger or poverty or cancer or global annihilation, or mere personal failure and disappointment and unhappiness, that nothing can be done and despair because of it. Or, she can reject fatalism. I hope she does not accept it; I hope she does not act as if any of those fates are just.

One of the courses in philosophy I took was centered around the question whether any particular one of us would be willing to kill. The answer to that is answered everyday in obvious ways in the newspaper. I think the real question is whether any one of us is willing to stand up and not be killed. She'ifa needs to become as irreplaceable to herself as she already is to me. She needs to believe *as if forever*.

She might make a difference. She might take responsibility for her world. She might choose nothing less than what the future is to be, and realize that her justification comes in the fact that she can do good. Maybe, she can have a more compassionate approach to life. Maybe, she can live with some conscious appreciation for the condition of the rest of the world. Maybe, she can see that human beings are good and act *as if she were good*.

In the end, this is what I know. I touch reality subjectively in my moral decisions. Detached speculations of reason, rationality, have their place, but they do not power an ethic. Faith powers an ethic: a belief in the power to create my own values, to hold them, to live them . . . But I must remember that this is the earth, my home: it is a tragically beautiful place and there is no sun without a shadow.

I give She'ifa a hug. The hug, the love: these too are starting points, places to occupy, anchorholds, a language that I can live in truthfully.